IMAGES
of America

LAUREL
COUNTY

UNION WORSHIP SERVICE
11:00 A. M.

COMMUNITY SINGING
2:00 P. M.

—o—

Official Opening

Levi Jackson Wilderness Road State Park

London, Ky.

Sunday, July 14th, 1935

—o—

Entrance off Dixie Highway, 3 miles south of London

ADMISSION FREE----NO FEES OF ANY KIND

Bring Picnic Dinner and Stay All Day

UNDER AUSPICES OF THE LONDON FIREMEN'S BAND
PROGRAM COMPLIMENTS OF THE SENTINEL-ECHO

IMAGES
of America

LAUREL
COUNTY

Carl Keith Greene

ARCADIA

First published 1997
Copyright © Carl Keith Greene, 1997

ISBN 0-7524-0808-9

Published by Arcadia Publishing,
an imprint of the Chalford Publishing Corporation,
One Washington Center, Dover, New Hampshire 03820.
Printed in Great Britain

Library of Congress Cataloging-in-Publication Data applied for

Contents

Program

Rev. R. P. Mahon In Charge.

Hymn—"All Hail the Power."
Prayer—Rev. W. S. Irvin.
Hymn—"What a Friend We Have in Jesus."
Announcements.
Sermon—Rev. Dr. R. J. Yoak, of Somerset.
Hymn—"I Love To Tell The Story."
Benediction—Rev. P. T. Smith.

Afternoon Song Service—2:00 o'clock.

London Firemen's Band, Sponsors.

Band Selection.
The Lord's Prayer, led by Rev. F. E. Sanders.
Song—"America."
    "Onward, Christian Soldiers."
    "Old Folks at Home."

Band Selection.
Song—"Flow Gently, Sweet Afton."
    "Darling Nellie Gray."
    "Annie Laurie."

Accordion Duet—Swiss Folk Tunes, by Mr. Adolph
    Sahli and Mrs. Ida Bertschinger.

Address—"Levi Jackson Wilderness Road State
    Park," by Hon. Nat B. Sewell.

Song—"When You and I Were Young, Maggie."
    "Carry Me Back to Old Virginny."
    "Stand Up. Stand Up for Jesus."

Mountain Ballad—"Barbara Allen," by Mrs. Nettie
    Johnson, Mrs. Nettie Sasser and Mrs.
    Millie Phelps

Song—"The Church in the Wildwood."
    "My Old Kentucky Home."
    "Sweet By and By."

Benediction—Rev. M. A. Jollay.

The entire audience will join in repeating The Lord's Prayer
and in singing all songs except as noted.

Introduction

A year ago, when Images of America: *London* was published, I realized that there were more photographs in my collection and probably more photographs in other families' collections that should be shared with others. So I decided to try a second book, a bit broader in scope, that would show scenes from all across the county, as well as include photographs of some of London and Laurel County citizens. I went through my own collection and came up with another large number of photographs, and I put the word out that I was looking for more old photographs. To my delight, many friends and acquaintances came through. This book, Images of America: *Laurel County*, is a result of the effort of many Laurel Countians, and I truly appreciate those who have contributed to the book. I simply could not have done it alone.

Laurel County has served as southeast Kentucky's hub since the settlers began coming through the Cumberland Gap on their way to the rolling bluegrass region, or the rich river bottomland along the Kentucky and Dix and Green Rivers.

In those days the travelers made their decision as to whether to go to Boonesboro or Crab Orchard when they arrived at Wood's Blockhouse at Hazel Patch where Skagg's Trace and the Wilderness Road diverged.

Today Laurel County still serves as the crossroads of Kentucky. Travelers use London and its main north-south, east-west highways to get where they are going, and soon, a rebuilt KY 30 will take travelers to the northeastern corner of the state in a more direct manner. And, if Congress funds a new interstate highway, I-66 will eventually pass somewhere near Laurel County and London, bringing visitors from western Virginia.

Laurel County was chosen after World War II by regional companies as the site of their new manufacturing plants and bakeries. Kern's Bakery located a facility here just after the war, and Knoxville Fertilizer Company built a plant here about the same time. Other national businesses saw what we had to offer and began building plants here.

Caron Spinning Company, Phoenix Manufacturing, American Greetings Corporation, and NCR, to name a few, located plants here. Laurel County, whose economy was based on diverse industries, fared much better than its neighbors as the coal-fed economy of the 1970s began to sputter.

A hundred years ago, two Methodist sisters from Richmond in Madison County had the dream to open a school somewhere in southeastern Kentucky. The search for a site included many of the towns surrounding London. Eventually, London was chosen as the site for Sue Bennett Memorial School, and London's status as an education center was established.

At about the same time, the federal judiciary began eyeing London, and soon, with the help of congressmen Vincent Boreing and D.C. Edwards, London was put on the circuit of the United States District Court for the Eastern District of Kentucky. A few years later a modern stone building designed to house the federal court and the U.S. Post Office was built.

In the early part of the 1950s, a makeshift aircraft landing strip was developed into a modern airport. Federal aviation authorities located their offices there as Piedmont Airlines began scheduled service to London, and that reportedly made London the smallest town in the country with regular airline service and regular airmail delivery.

Geographers predict that when the year 2000 census is taken and Laurel Countians are officially counted, Laurel County will be among the three or four fastest growing counties in the state.

This book is dedicated to the memory of those who have helped develop Laurel into the leading county in southeast Kentucky—from Titus Mershon to John Wood, from Lot Pitman and John Jackson (who furnished the room where the county was organized and named) to Levi Jackson and his father-in-law, John Freeman; from D.C. Edwards and Vincent Boreing to William Randall to William Lewis to Finley Hamilton; from Drs. J.B. Mason and H.V., Walter, and Robert Pennington, to Drs. Sam Adams and Boyce Jones; from Fred Lucas to Chester Scoville; from J.W. Stevenson to Russell and Martin Dyche; from "Cheap" John Pearl to the Hackney brothers and Robert Parman; and from Prof. H.V. McClure and J.C. Lewis to W.B. Hall.

The book is also dedicated to those Laurel Countians, all the names of which we'll never know, who worked their small farms, toiled in retail establishments and factories, operated their "mom and pop" businesses, paid taxes, supported the schools and churches, voted for the better person, buried the dead, cut the lumber, dug the coal, built the homes and businesses and roads, sacrificed for their children, taught those children, healed the ills and wounds of Laurel's citizens, prayed for their souls, fought their battles in the wars, and made Laurel County what it is today.

In the following pages, you'll find images from London's past as well as scenes from communities around the county. You'll see faces of those who were influential as politicians, business people, educators, firefighters, and lawmen. You'll also find the faces of Laurel Countians who were not so famous or influential, but who were important to the development and vitality of Laurel County nonetheless.

I also dedicate this book to the memory of my parents, Carl G. and Daisy Greene, who encouraged my interest in historical research and photography, and to my grandparents, John and Lou Miller and W.T. and America Greene, who helped me to understand the families from which I came and to appreciate the work of my forebears, who carved homes and cities out of the wilderness and developed this county into a vital community.

So, now, take another look at London and Laurel County's past and have a chance to walk there, with them, again.

One
Faces in Laurel

There are several families in Laurel County that have been here for generations; many of those families' roots dip deeply into Laurel's history, perhaps as far back as the founding of the county in 1826. One of these old families is the Scoville family, shown above. Pauline Pigg Scoville (seated in the center) is the mother of (clockwise from front left) Frances Scoville Jones, Mary Scoville Swaner, Helen Scoville Caley, Elizabeth Scoville, Hallie Mae Scoville White, Magnolia Scoville, and Nora Scoville McWhorter. It is known that at least two of these women, Mary and Hallie Mae, lived more than a century. Their brothers were Hector, John, and Warren Scoville. Pauline Pigg Scoville's husband was Sheldon.

John Paul Jones and Polly Pigg were photographed on the front steps of London High School in the 1940s.

The late Minnie Black, who lived on KY 30 just east of East Bernstadt, was a crafter of gourds. She made characters, musical instruments, and even animals from the gourds. She is shown here playing a gourd harp for a London Lions Club meeting in the 1980s. Black is the only Laurel Countian to date to have appeared on both *The Tonight Show* with Johnny Carson and David Letterman's late-night television show. She displayed her gourds and roundly upstaged both Carson and Letterman, to the delight of both comedians.

Thelma Black posed on March 3, 1922, near the Laurel County Poor Farm on Whitley Street.

About the same year, Lester V. Roper posed with a dump truck apparently owned by J.W. Brannan Sand and Gravel Company.

The Laurel County Fiscal Court was photographed in the early 1970s. They are, from left to right: (front row) Onas Patton, Glenn Robbins, Tom Monhollon, James Walden, Larry Black, and Ed Parsley; (second row) County Clerk Henry Walden, County Executive Ledford Karr, and County Attorney Elmer Cunnagin.

Members of London's City Council were photographed in January 1960. Mayor George Sutton is seated and behind him are, from left to right: Herman House, Ted Jody, Floyd Robinson, Luther Harville, Leslie Sparks, and Howard Jones (with a bandaged face).

London merchant Wayne Reep supervised the reconstruction of his business after a large portion of East Fourth Street was devastated by an explosion and fire in January 1978. The fire damaged most of the block east of Main Street, but the only injuries were to passers-by in automobiles who were struck by flying debris. (From the collection of Linda Wayne Reep.)

Bob Herron (left) and Joe Havens (right) discussed the news of the day in Havens's office at London Dry Goods Company in the 1970s. London Dry Goods was one of the first wholesale companies to locate in London in modern times. It was in business until the early 1980s. (From the collection of Don Chesnut.)

(**Left**) Oliver Harrison is seen here working on a shoe sometime in the 1970s in his shoe repair shop on the corner of East Fifth and Hill Streets. Harrison spent most of his life in the shoe business, having established the company in the 1930s. He retired a few years before his death. (**Below**) Harrison shares a moment with Wayne Reep (right), who operated the furniture store opened at about the same time Harrison went into business. (From the collection of Don Chesnut.)

Gene Chadwell was photographed inside the Standard Oil station that he operated on East Fourth Street.

Paul "Bud" Ott is shown in the general store that he and his family operated for many years at Bernstadt, Kentucky, a community colonized by the Swiss in the 1880s. (From the collection of Don Chesnut.)

Ernest "Preacher" Blair posed in the early 1980s at his auto parts business on East Fourth Street. The building was about to be razed to make room for a new building Blair had built for the business. The stone building shown here was built more than fifty years earlier and served for a time as a liquor store until Prohibition closed it along with all the other legal whisky outlets in London, as well as the nation.

Richard Riley, one of London High's outstanding football and basketball players, is shown here in about 1966. Riley was named Best Athlete for the 1966/67 term at London High. He was all-state and all-conference in football, scoring a school record 173 points for the year. In basketball, he was named all-district and honorable mention all-state, and he held the school record of total career points scored. He also played baseball and ran track.

Margaret and Ernest Porter posed in 1934 somewhere in the Fariston community south of London. The Porters were in the grocery business in London for half a century. Porter's store stood on the corner of East Fourth and McWhorter Streets until the 1980s, when the times forced them to build a new, larger, more modern store across East Fourth Street from the first store. The Porters' daughter and son-in-law, Ernestine and Kenneth House, helped with the store until two of their children, Stuart and Ernest Matt, took over the business. The third grandson, Brian House, is a lawyer in London, and he supplied this photograph.

The problem of having to open the valve at the bottom of a slender, drilled-well bucket by hand—the result being a wet (and in the winter, cold) hand—sent the young W.S. Carpenter to the drawing board during the Depression, and a new bucket with a bail that opened the valve from the top was invented. After patenting the design, he began producing it at the London Bucket Company in London, which adapted to the modern times by adding a sheet-metal shop, a heating and cooling shop, and a plumbing supply house as drilled wells began to disappear. The company, founded in 1931, closed in the early 1980s.

Dyche Jones was a well-known figure in London for much of his professional life. He was music director at First Baptist Church, elected governor of the Kiwanis Club's Kentucky-Tennessee District, and the operator of a small chain of food stores named for him. Jones and his wife recently moved to Richmond to be near their son, Bill Frank, and his family.

Rose McHargue (seen here) and her husband, Delbert, operated a clothing store on South Main Street for many years.

Cecil Yeary, a Middlesboro native, was the operator of the London Insurance Company until his retirement. Yeary was active in Kiwanis Club and the London-Laurel County Development Association. He was married to the former Daisy Engle.

19

The late Earl Wallace came to London as a student at Sue Bennett Memorial School, learned his lessons, and went on to bigger and better things with the Standard Oil Company. In his later years, he became a major benefactor of Sue Bennett College and its alumni association, and he also contributed major funding to the production of Dr. Thomas Clark's history of Laurel County, published by the Laurel County Historical Society. Here he is seen at a historical society meeting with Lucy Dillion, who retired as librarian at London High School before her death. In the background is Penny Ferguson.

Roscoe Mason was a fixture in downtown London in the 1950s and 1960s. His grin and greetings won him friends among the merchants and townspeople who were regulars at the downtown eateries. Though he was a bit slow of wit, he was beloved by all to whom he befriended. He loved children and they loved him. In the days before state and federally subsidized healthcare, the physicians and dentists in town took care of his needs *pro bono*. This photograph was made at the 1964 Laurel County Homecoming.

Russell Dyche was editor and publisher of London's *Sentinel-Echo* for more than fifty years, having merged the *Mountain Echo* and the *London Sentinel*. Dyche also served as head of the Kentucky State Park System and was instrumental with Lee McHargue and others in establishing the Levi Jackson Wilderness Road State Park. He promoted the establishment of the Laurel County Homecoming (the oldest annual event of its kind in the state), started the city's water system, and was an outspoken editorialist, championing long and hard the causes he espoused.

Russell Dyche's son, Martin (left), took over the reins of the newspaper at his father's retirement. Here he is seen with Col. Harland Sanders and Sanders's wife, Claudia. Sanders opened the restaurant where he cooked and served his first batch of Kentucky Fried Chicken in southern Laurel County.

The Begley Drug Company was established in London in the 1920s and flourished as a small chain of drugstores, pharmacies, and dry cleaners throughout Kentucky and for a short time in Mississippi before it was bought by the Rite Aid Corporation in the early 1980s. Shown above are some of the employees of the London stores at an awards presentation. From left to right are Paul Evans (a district supervisor), Harry W. Houchens, Donna Disney, Robert Begley (a founder of the corporation and its president), Daisy Greene, Mike Morton, and Bobby Begley (an officer of the corporation). (From the collection of Wilma Houchens.)

At an earlier awards meeting are, from left to right: Elmer Browning, Hazel Banks, Jessie Chandler, Robert Begley, Harry Houchens, Wilma Houchens, Irene Spurlock, Carl G. Greene, Gillis Gregory and Bill Begley. Not shown in either photograph are long-time employees Gene Champion, Gerry Sutton, Lottie Smith, and Maude Brown. (From the collection of Wilma Houchens.)

In the days before air conditioning, the front porch was often the summer refuge of families for fresh, if not so cool, air. These four families chose the front porch of a duplex apartment house on College Street. (Above) Pictured, from left to right, are as follows: Carl G. Greene and his son Carl Keith, Glenn Chaney, Lester Finley, and Cecil Byrd. (Below) From left to right are: Lorene Byrd; young master Greene and his mother, Daisy; Billie Chaney and her daughter, Kathy; and Margie Finley. The Greenes and Chaneys lived in the two apartments around 1953. (From the collection of Lorene Byrd.)

This photograph of the family of B. Robert "Bert" Stivers was made sometime in the 1960s. Shown on his father's knee, Robert Stivers is now a lawyer and state senator. From left to right, Bert Stivers (seated in the arm chair) served as circuit judge for Knox and Laurel Counties; Mary Beth is now a tenured professor of Home Economics at Middle Tennessee State University in Murfreesboro; Franklin is a lawyer and former president of the local bar association; Louise is dean of students at Upper Iowa University in Fayette; and their mother, Joan, was a longtime instructor and administrator at Sue Bennett College and served three years as its president.

The Elijah T. Cornett family was photographed sometime in the 1950s. Shown, from left to right, are as follows: (seated in the swing) Elijah T. Cornett, Bernice Cornett, and Polly Hall Cornett; (standing) Grace, Kermit, Ruby, Larkin, Pearly, Ora, Lawrence, Clorissa, and Avis.

The Hackney family has had a large place in Laurel County's history. Shown on the fiftieth wedding anniversary of Edwin H. Hackney Sr. and Helen Pearl Hackney, August 15, 1933, is nearly all the family in London at the time. From left to right, members of the family are listed as identified on the back of the photograph: (first row) Kate Faris Pearl, Sallie Pearl Lucas, William Hackney who is holding Thomas Ward Myers, Helen Pearl Hackney holding Helen Irene Hackney, Edwin Hobbs Hackney Sr. holding Margaret Sue Hackney, Sue Dunlap Hackney, Stella Brown Stith, and Ruby H. Carnahan; (second row) Chris Pearl, Edna Pearl Hackney Post, Eugene Williams Hackney, Louise Horrine Hackney, W.R. Champion, Edwin Hobbs Hackney Jr., Willis Granville Hackney, Harry Murray, Malena Murray Hackney, Madge Eversole Hackney, and Louise Winterburg Hackney; (third row) Hazel H. Pearl, Edith Crosby Hackney Myers, Martha Pearl, Jacob Ward Hackney, Lois Pearl Champion, Horace Brown Hackney, Glennie Tipper Hackney, Frances Myers, John Lawrence Hackney, Charlie Pearl, William Christopher Hackney, Aleene Hackney, Wells Dalton, and Mary Brown Coldwell. The photograph was taken by P.L. Young at the Hackney home on West First Street. (From the collection of Irene Isaacs.)

Helen Pearl and E.H. Hackney Sr. posed for this picture a few years later. He is sporting the bowler hat that London's people were accustomed to seeing. The Hackneys were active in the mercantile business in London, having operated a department store for nearly a hundred years from 1879. It was billed as "where your grandfather traded." (From the collection of Irene Isaacs.)

Jacob Hackney, the father of E.H. Hackney Sr., joined his son in the mercantile business in 1882. (From the collection of Irene Isaacs.)

Willis G. Hackney, Jacob's grandson, is shown in the early days of World War II at Fort Riley, Kansas. Willis Hackney was the commander of the Kentucky Home Guard's Cavalry Troop in London when it was activated for the war. After riding their horses to the depot and loading themselves and the livestock on the train, the troop was retrained as a coast artillery battery and saw duty in the European theater. Willis came home, became manager of the department store, and held that post until his death in 1968. (From the collection of Irene Isaacs.)

This troop of Brownie Scouts was eager to get to work toward "flying up" to Girl Scouts. Pictured, from left to right, the Brownies were as follows: (first row) unknown, Kay Humfleet, Candy Howard, Libby Isaacs, Louise Isaacs, and unknown; (second row) Linda Jones, Barbara Seeley, Susan Phelps, Michelle Milby, Monica Adams, and Mary Dupree; (third row) unknown, Doris Douglas, and Terry Timberlake. (From the collection of Irene Isaacs.)

Another troop of Brownies, which could not be identified for this book, was photographed in the mechanical area of the Sentinel-Echo plant, sometime around 1960.

This photograph of the Hazel Green Elementary School's seventh grade class was made in 1957. (From the collection of Carolyn Harris.)

The London School band was photographed in front of the band hall in the 1953/54 school year. Band members are, from left to right, as follows: (front row) Sue Feltner, Billie Shomaker, Bill Eversole, Luann Dunaway (clarinetists), Joyce Jones (oboist), Sue Black (bassoonist), Betty Ann House, and Barbara Bird (flutists); (second row) Beverly Campbell, Polly Bruner, Judy Weaver, Dumpy Smith, Ann Mullins, Leo Phillips, Jimmie Parsley, Jean Raefield (clarinetists), Barbara Dobbs, Judy Williams, Julia Hodges (French hornists), Tommy Harris, Jimmy Barton, Bobbie Jones, and Bobby J. Ennslin (saxophonists); (third row) Donna Walters, Jean McNeece, Jean Ann Barton, Peggy Dobbs, Wiletta Harrison, Florence Holt (clarinetists), Byron Thompson, Ed Taylor, Gary Vaughn, Bill Chesnut, Tommy Walters, Janice Brown (cornetists), Walter Moss, Shirley "Sweetie" Acton, Raymond Asher, and Paul Sizemore (saxophonists); (back row) Mary Ann Jones, Joan Kidd (percussionists), Don Hacker (director), Joe Hiller, Richard Harper (sousaphonists), William Sizemore, Walter Barnett, Walter Thompson, Betty Draper, Jackie Barrett (percussionists), George Johnson, Jimmy Jones (baritone hornists), Eldon Phillips, Ted Brown, Tom Craft, and Matt Sutton (trombonists). (From the collection of Sweetie Smith.)

The Hob Nob Cafe was one of the hangouts for London High School students in the early 1950s. This view shows the interior of the restaurant and its owner at the time, Obert Acton. (From the collection of Sweetie Smith.)

Hanging out in front of the Hob Nob in about 1952 are, from left to right, Shirley "Sweetie" Acton (now Smith), Barbara Bird (Pennington), Wanda Peace (Marcum), and Jackie Barrett (Ball). Sweetie Acton's father was the owner of the cafe. (From the collection of Sweetie Smith.)

Also shown in front of the Hob Nob are Matilda Reynolds, her daughters Marie Reynolds Acton (left center) and Maude Reynolds Brown (right center), Mrs. Brown's son Joe, and his younger brother, Ted. (From the collection of Sweetie Smith.)

In about 1910 Lillie Moore and her sister, Tommie Bryant (seated), posed for a cameraman. Among the children of Lillie Moore are Hazel Banks, Bill Moore, Edith Kelly, Beulah May, Dorothy Bolton, and Jim Moore. (From the collection of Terry House.)

Lillie Moore's son, eighteen-year-old Private Bill Moore, posed for an army photographer soon after completing his basic training. Bill Moore became a Shell Oil dealer after completing his military obligation, and he eventually became a Goodyear dealer. His London Tire Center is still in operation under the management of his son, also named Bill, and daughter, Terry House. (From the collection of Terry House.)

Bill Moore and his wife, Eulene, now a retired teacher from the Laurel County school system, are avid fishers. This November 4, 1960 photograph of Mrs. Moore shows just how good she is with a fishing pole. (From the collection of Terry House.)

Hazel and Edison Banks celebrated their wedding day, June 14, 1952, by cutting the wedding cake. Hazel is Bill Moore's sister, and she currently operates a catering service. She operated a successful restaurant for many years and before that, was a clerk at Begley Drug. Mr. Banks is a retired agriculture instructor in the Laurel County school system. (From the collection of Terry House.)

For the eleven years before 1928, John L. Bruner was a professional baseball player, and a southpaw pitcher to boot. Here he is shown in uniform for the Quincy, Indiana team. After completing college in 1916, he joined the Philadelphia Athletics. A year later he joined the Army Air Service and served as a balloon commander until 1918. After the war, he returned to professional baseball, and when he left the field, he was playing for the Newport News, Virginia team. Upon returning to Laurel County, he went to work at the East Bernstadt Bank and eventually opened an insurance agency in London. In about 1938 he married Mable Casteel, and they had four children, Coralie, Billie Bryan, Jack Casteel, and John Lee Jr. (From the collection of Coralie Young.)

John Bruner's mother, Laura Bruner, is shown with some of her children and grandchildren at the family home on North Main Street. Standing in front of the home, from left to right, are: (front row) Billie Bryan Bruner, Coralie Bruner, Beatrice "Sis" Bruner, Jack Casteel Bruner, and Betty Jo Bruner; (back row) Milroy Bruner, Philip Hodge, Laura Bruner, Bill Bruner, and Laura Lee Hamilton. In the background, to the right, are Lillie Hamilton and John Bruner. (From the collection of Coralie Young.)

Finley Hamilton was the only Democrat from Laurel County to be elected to the U.S. Congress. He was elected and served a two-year term. His election came in a statewide at-large election in 1932. Other congressmen from Laurel County include W.R. Randall, Vincent Boreing, Don C. Edwards, and William Lewis. (From the collection of Coralie Young.)

C.A. Casteel was a merchant and farmer in the 1920s and 1930s on a huge farm north of East Bernstadt on what is now KY 490. This photograph shows him on the farm on the bridge that led to the boathouse in the middle of his pond. (From the collection of Coralie Young.)

Dr. Mac Whitis was a physician who practiced in East Bernstadt for many years. This photograph shows Whitis (right) with Wilson Casteel. Both men were well-known citizens of the community north of London.

Dr. Chester Tyree graduated from the University of Louisville Dental School in 1909. Soon after that, he married Stella Eversole. He was eighty-two years old when he died. Tyree was one of London's first modern dentists. He even took a portable dental chair to Bond in Jackson County once a week to treat the lumber workers there. Marbeth Craft and Chesney Eversole are the surviving children of Chester and Stella Tyree. Marbeth remembered her father as a man interested in sports and travel. She particularly remembered one summer when the family took a trip to Whitesburg in a "big touring car" and had eighteen flat tires on the way. The Tyrees' other children were Louise Blue, Sam, and Frank. (From the collection of Susan Tyree.)

Rufus J. Bruner Sr. posed with his wife, Golden Casteel, at her father's farm near Altamont on what is now KY 490, north of East Bernstadt. This photograph was made in 1934.

Dr. Sam Tyree joined his father in the practice of dentistry when he graduated from the University of Louisville Dental School in 1946. The two practiced together until his father's death, and Sam maintained the practice. He was an avid hunter and fisherman and served on London's city council longer than any other council member. He died in 1995. This photograph was made probably at the time of his graduation from dental school. He and his wife, Evelyn, had two children, Laura Susan and Norman Chester. (From the collection of Susan Tyree.)

R.J. Bruner Sr. served in the infantry during World War I. He told a *Sentinel-Echo* reporter in 1954 that he missed seeing action by the skin of his teeth. He and his brother, John L., had more than World War I service in common. They married sisters, Golden and Mable Casteel.

In the spring of 1945 two brothers, both World War I veterans, and their brother-in-law welcomed Clyde Jones (right) home. From left to right are John Bruner, Russell Bowman, and Rufus J. Bruner Sr. (From the collection of R.J. Bruner Jr.)

Margaret Jones was one of London's children who went away and made good. She was a dancer, and her feet took her to New York and Europe and on tours of the South and East. She even had her own television show in the early 1950s, when television was in its infancy. She retired to London and joined her sister, Catherine, in the family home after leaving the stage. She then began teaching dance to London's children. She was an accomplished ballerina and specialized in East Indian dance. (From the collection of Ron Ingram.)

Ottis Ingram and his wife, Lillian, operated Ballard's Dining Room on North Main, opposite the Christian Church, for twenty-two years beginning in 1952. Here Ottis is shown making his way down East Seventh Street. Behind him can be seen a portion of the Martin Cupp and Son Furniture Company. Ballard's, founded by Pauline Ballard, was one of London's most popular eateries, with banquet rooms and space for meetings of groups such as the Kiwanis and Lions Clubs. Downtown London once had such a plethora of restaurants that nearly each block had its own place to eat. (From the collection of Ron Ingram.)

In the first Dyche Jones Food Store on Broad Street in the late 1950s, the stock men included the following students (from left to right): Richie Hamm, Bill Hill, Craig Whitlock, Hershel Corne, and Bill Frank Jones. Note the neon Kentucky Ice Cream sign (upper right). (From the collection of Geedle Jody Peters.)

At a meeting of the minds at London Electric in the early 1950s, a photographer caught the following group (from left to right): (standing) Jack Phelps, his brother J.B., Calloway Blevins, and Gilmore (a third Phelps brother); (seated) Ron Ingram and Gilmore Phelps's son, Fred. (From the collection of Ron Ingram.)

Murray L. Brown practiced law in London for about forty years, beginning in about 1940. He was a native of western Kentucky and practiced law there before being appointed commonwealth's attorney for Clay County. He left the prosecutor's position and came to London in about 1940, reportedly after the Clay County sheriff, with whom he had walked out of the Clay County Courthouse, was gunned down in an ambush. (From the collection of Tooms and House.)

A.E. "Gene" Smith (left) points out a landmark as he, Jake Whittenback (center), and an architect discuss the layout of the "back nine" at the London Country Club. Smith was a local businessman and former president of the country club. (From the collection of Sweetie Smith.)

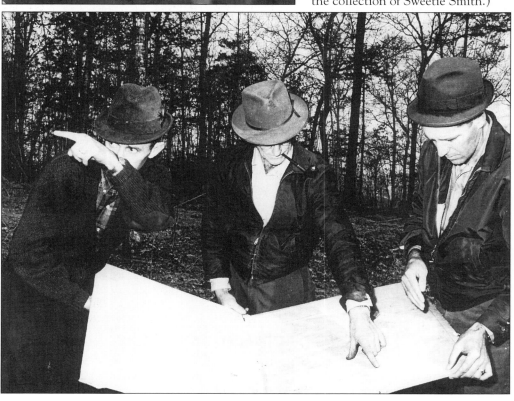

Two
Life in Laurel

In the days before political correctness, *Brown v. Board of Education,* and the events that changed the course of history in Selma, Montgomery, and Memphis, minstrel shows were a popular form of entertainment. The London Lions Club produced several of the shows in the 1950s. This photograph, probably from the 1951 show, includes, from left to right, (standing) Helen Rose Dyche, Billie Bryan Bruner, and her mother, Mable, as a trio. Also shown are Sue Buchanan (seated, between the Bruners), and Dobbie Magee and Bill Bruner (seated on the extreme right). Bruner served as the "interlocutor." (From the collection of Iris Higgs.)

The London Lions Club's jug band was featured at other events besides the minstrel shows. From left to right are (probably) J.C. Doane (with jug), Charlie Higgs (with washtub bass), Billy Russell (with guitar), and Harry Snyder (on trumpet). The three men on the right could not be identified. Bill Bruner holds the microphone for Higgs's bass solo. (From the collection of Iris Higgs.)

At what may have been the 1954 version of the minstrel show was a trio that appears to include Sue Buchanan (center), Billie Bryan Bruner (right), and a lady at the left who could not be identified. In the background appears to be Barbara Robinson (left), Bill Bruner (with white cap), and Judy Williams (in dance outfit). (From the collection of Iris Higgs.)

The format of the minstrel shows included a "fashion show," often peopled by models wearing the clothing of the opposite gender. This photograph from the 1951 show identifies this model as Ed Hackney, who carries a sign proclaiming that his (her?) girdle was provided by Mary Terry. (From the collection of Coralie Young.)

This photograph, labeled "The Best End Men," identifies these three minstrels, from left to right, as Rufus Bruner, Jim Bowles, and Bob May. The minstrel shows were major fund-raisers for the Lions Club, and they were alternated between the Reda Theatre stage and a stage of the Southland Theatre before it burned. Many local entertainers had their first shot at public performances in the minstrel shows. (From the collection of R.J. Bruner.)

Joe Owens (standing at right) is the only person who could be identified in the photograph from his collection. Perhaps the man on the mule was a member of the London Home Guard, which was a cavalry unit.

London's Home Guard was known across the state for the quality of its mounted drill team. This photograph from the Irene Isaacs collection shows part of the unit drilling sometime before World War II.

(Above) This second photograph of the Home Guard cavalry unit shows more drill practice. When the London unit of the Home Guard (by then part of the National Guard) was called for duty in World War II, it rode in mounted procession to the railroad station. (Below) This photograph shows a troop train at the London station, perhaps at the beginning of World War II. (Both from the collection of Irene Isaacs.)

Mounted and ready to go with the London Home Guard was Lt. Rufus J. Bruner Sr., a veteran of World War I. This photograph was made in about 1920. (From the collection of R.J. Bruner Jr.)

The London Home Guard posed at Straight Creek in Harlan County in 1923. The unit was activated several times during that era to help quell violence during United Mine Workers strikes in the mountains. (From the collection of R.J. Bruner Jr.)

Life in Laurel in the good old days was not so good that meat could be put on the table as the result of a short trip to the market. In fact, in the early part of the century, many Laurel Countians were still raising and slaughtering their own beef and pork. These photographs show a hog killing on the F.M. "Mack" Barnett farm west of London.

Little Falls, a small waterfall that drops about 50 feet, is located on property now owned by Elmo Greer just off Parker Road. For years the falls and the surrounding area were the playground for London's young people. This photograph from the 1920s shows two of London's young ladies on the rocks that jut out above the pool at Little Falls. No one could identify the ladies in this photograph from the Irene Isaacs collection.

In 1926 the eighth grade team at East Bernstadt School won the county championship. From left to right are Euley Harrison, Wilson Casteel, Johnny Cromer, Edgar Luker, J.W. Crook (principal and coach), Arvil Farmer, Fred Phelps, and Walter Adams. (From the collection of R.J. Bruner Jr.)

52

Sometime in about 1923 or 1924, the Berean Sunday School Class at London's First Baptist Church fielded a baseball team. Players include the following: (front row) Red Robbins, Beck Young, Roy Cottongim, George Hamm, Elmer Williams, and John Estes; (back row) Bill Young, Everette Nicholson, Bob Williams, Charlie Crawford, Red Walden, Rufus J. Bruner Sr., and Charles Baugh. Bob Hamm is one of the boys shown looking over the shoulders of Bruner and Baugh; the other couldn't be identified. (From the collection of R.J. Bruner Jr.)

The Laurel County Board of Education offered what we now call "continuing education" in the 1920s. This photograph, made on the front steps of the old Laurel County Courthouse, shows the participants in a teachers' institute.

The 1940 Hazel Green High School baseball team posed with coach Clark E. Chesnut. Chesnut was outstanding as a coach at Hazel Green for many years, particularly in tennis. The school was the only high school in the county with a permanent tennis court until consolidation. The players are, from left to right: (front row) Raymond McWhorter, J.B. Parsley, Marvin McWhorter, and Roy McWhorter; (back row) Alva Bowman, Albert Elza, Charles McDaniel, Coach Chesnut, Darrell Parsley, Raymond Anders, and Nolan Moren. (From the collection of Raymond Harris.)

This shot was simply labeled "Hazel Green Class." It appears to be from the 1930s or 1940s and was probably an elementary school class. (From the collection of Raymond Harris.)

In around 1958 London City School Superintendent Lloyd B. Cox (left) prepares to present a diploma to a London High coed. Neither she nor the two seated men were identified.

Though small, with an average of about 350 students, London High had a dynamic music program. The school's chorus under the direction of Mildred Cutshaw is seen here performing in the school gymnasium in about 1958.

In a photograph made at the same concert, Miss Cutshaw is shown with the London High concert band. The London School Band was organized in the 1930s by the London Firemen's Club as a successor to the club's band. The firemen's band was a fine training ground for young musicians, and under John Griffey's direction, the London School Band flourished. The London High band, along with its elementary music program, has seen some outstanding directors since Griffey, including Wilma Pigg Poynter, Don Hacker, Ray Tingle, Wes Kirby, Mildred Cutshaw, Beth Dejong, John Patrick, and Jack McCarty.

London High had some dedicated academic instructors as well. Shown here from about 1963 are Miss Tradathan Estes (right) and student Anetta Boggs discussing a term paper. Miss Estes had been an instructor since World War II, and she retired at the close of the 1963/64 school year.

Life in Laurel County in the 1950s for teenagers included trips to Levi Jackson Park (but good girls never went there after dark), the London Drive-In with its Richardson's Root Beer sign on the roof, and the Reda Theatre (and the Reda Drive-In and Ronnie Drive-In Theatre). This birthday party group that includes Glen Doyle, Barbara Carter, and Geedle Jody was planning to celebrate at the Ocean Wave Skating Rink at Fariston. (From the collection of Geedle Jody Peters.)

A few years earlier, only girls were invited to this birthday party in about 1953. The picture was made in front of the first St. William Elementary School on Broad Street. From left to right are Mary Catherine Boone, Frances Boone, Geedle Jody, Sandra Sparks, Lois Ann Blunschi, Mary Louise O'Neal, and Geraldine O'Neal. (From the collection of Geedle Jody Peters.)

In the "good old days" it was the barber shop where London's men hung out, not only for tonsorial services, but to discuss the news of the day or to just kick back and read the paper or maybe cat-nap in a chair. The photographs on this page are from about 1922. **(Above)** According to the window sign, this is the Neal Hundley Barber Shop, in the north end of the Catching Building, about the northeast corner of Main and Fourth Streets. The Jackson Building, now housing a law office and insurance company, can be seen through the window. The only identified person is Rufus Bruner (barber, standing behind center chair). **(Below)** This photograph looks into Bill Fouts's shop. Pictured are: (first chair) Roscoe Estep (barber) with customer Jim Pigg; (second chair) Rufus Bruner (barber) with John Hackney; (third chair) Charles Hicks (barber) with Jim Robinson; (fourth chair) Bill Fouts (barber) with an unidentified girl; (fifth chair) Charles Crawford. The shoeshine man is Bob Beaty. (Both from the collection of R.J. Bruner Jr.)

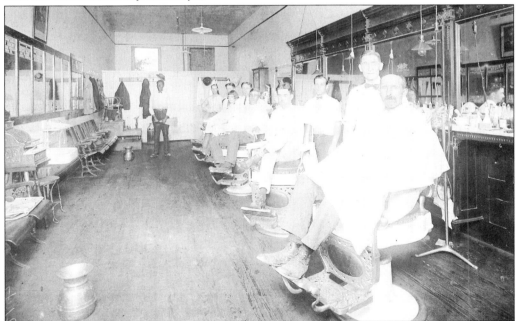

The Sue Bennett Memorial School (SBMS) came to town about a hundred years ago and brought some outstanding educators to instruct the children who were brought here to live and learn. This photograph shows the first set of instructors at the college in 1898. They are, from left to right, as follows: (seated) Florence Campbell, Superintendent J.C. Lewis, and Lilly Letton; (standing) Elizabeth Beaumont, J.W. Carnahan, Lucy Mahan, Mable Osborn, and B.F. Lawhorn.

This photograph taken at SBMS was made sometime before 1902. Sue Bennett was a school for elementary students in its early life, eventually establishing a high school, then a junior college, and finally a four-year college in the 1990s. It kept a training school for elementary students into the 1950s to allow its education majors to observe classroom instruction. These people, as listed on back of the photograph, are: (front row) Bertie Jackson, Mattie Pitman, unknown, Maggie Oakley, ? Barnes, unknown, and Hope Pitman, Florence Lewis, Edna Jackson, Ramie Steele and ? Oakley; (top row) Miss Beaumont, Prof. Lewis, Maria Stapleton, unknown, Bess Hackney, Bertie Thomson, unknown, Etta Mae Moore, Jade Bills, unknown, Vincent Yaden, unknown, ? Pitman, ? Saunders, ? Posey, unknown, Willie McKee, George Lewis, unknown, Clyde Ramsey and unknown. (From the archives of Sue Bennett College.)

By 1918 there were seniors graduating from the high school at SBMS. This photograph of that class includes, as listed on the back of the photograph: (front row) Jessie Parkins, Merle Wimberly, Lois Pearl, ? Stallings, and Mary Harkleroad; (second row) unknown, Beulah Stilwell, and unknown; (standing women) Catherine Pennington, Edith Hackney, and Kathleen Jones; (back row) Bill Norman, Oscar Parman, Dan Baugh, Harry Jones, John Raymer and Astor Hogg. (From the archives of Sue Bennett College.)

The school's thespians performed *Death Takes a Holiday* in 1938. Actors, from left to right, are as follows: (standing) Eddie Johnson, Fred McHargue, Mae Hardigree, Lynn Felts, Virginia Hutchinson, Billy Beam, Robert Stinson, Luther Gilley, and Eugene Meece; (seated) Desrie Thompson and Joyce Cunningham. (From the archives of Sue Bennett College.)

The high school class at Sue Bennett had grown by 1935. This class of seniors is identified as, from left to right: (front row) Julia Dixon, Dorothy Gregory, Mattie Sallee, Ruth Hilton, Maurine Johnston, Helen Crain, Eula Hopper, Erma Spence, Freda Trosper, Hazel Walker, and Ollie Gregory; (second row) Mary Mae Brock, Ona Mae Bailey, Thelma Jones, William Bianco, George Sasser, Ester Lee Hill, Chester Jones, Daisy Black, Charles Brown, and Mary V. Wilson; (third row) Ruby Tallent, Luther Depew, Ruth Williams, Sally Riley Harkleroad, Gertrude Baird, Ella M. Johnson, Beatrice Moore, Evelyn Watkins, Hazel Olinger, and Ruby Browning; (fourth row) Emma Lois Dickey, Estill Cornett, Sterling Perkins, Walter McDaniel, David Gregory, Hester Abner, Mable Isaacs, Cathleen Edens, Rosamond Johnson, Christine Faris, Lillian Gilbert, and Joe Gilbert; (back row) Delvin Holt, Earl Faris, John K. Lewis, and Robert Anderson. (From the archives of Sue Bennett College.)

This photograph of the entire student body at Sue Bennett (by then a junior college) on December 1, 1938, carried no other identification, though there are Hazel Green High letter sweaters visible on some of the men. (From the archives of Sue Bennett College.)

Crowning of the Queen of the May may have been derived from the Roman Catholic ritual of crowning the statue of the Blessed Virgin Mary each spring. These May Day activities at Sue Bennett were about ten years apart. **(Above)** This picture from the Sue Bennett College archives shows a May Queen and her court, either in 1928 or 1929. The stage may be what was left of the men's dormitory after it burned. The cellar and concrete floor remained near the school's tennis courts into the 1960s. **(Below)** This photograph from the Irene Isaacs collection shows a May Pole dance on the campus sometime in the 1940s.

On December 1, 1938, Miss Cathy Belle Motley's class at the SBC training school was photographed. From left to right are: (first row) Buddy Westbrook, Judy Matthews, Jack Harkleroad, Sue Hackney, Robert Wickersham, Betty Sue Cornett, Pat Powers, Randall Hubbard, Delores Clay, and Jimmy Whitaker; (second row) Scribner Goode, Margaret Ann Cook, Charles Owens, Geraldine Blair, Polly Pigg, Margaret Ellen Black, Irene Hackney, Ruth Owens, and Georgia Helen Rawlings; (third row) Jimmie Cook, Joe Davidson, Bobby Matthews, Betty Joe Williams, Doris Feltner, Martha Alice Gillian, Edward Wathen, and John Parman; (fourth row) Billie Jean McKeenan, Lois Marie Mansburger, Miss Motley (teacher), Harold Hubbard, and Lena Ruth Williams.

By 1942 the students above had entered Mrs. Wells's class. Students were, from left to right: (bottom row) Marcia Lee Smith, Geraldine Blair, Irene Hackney, Judy Matthews, Sue Hackney, Ruth Owens, Jay Davidson, Ray Reams, Bobby Murphy, and Jimmy Whitaker; (middle row) Edward Wathen, Bobby Mathews, Buddy Westbrook, Doris Feltner, Betty Joe Williams, Gladys Scott, John Parman, James Dew, and Jimmy Cook; (top row) Amazon Bill, John Watts, Jack Parman, Harold Hubbard, Dorothy Magee, Billy Gene McKeehan, Betty Smith, Loyd Buchanan, Billy Elliot, Patricia Lackey, Louise Johnson, Coralie Bruner, Lena Ruth Williams, and Mrs. Wells. (From the collection of Irene Hackney.)

Training school instructor Nora Johnson Clark is shown on the porch of one of the cottages that housed the training school in about 1941. She was a native of the western part of Laurel County and eventually left London to teach "somewhere out West," according to Irene Isaacs, from whose collection the photograph comes.

Memorial Hall at Sue Bennett, the men's dormitory shown in this postcard view made by Eberhart Studio in London, burned in 1925. The postcard was postmarked 1913 and was sent to a Bradfordsville, Kentucky man from a girl who was a student and signed the card, "Your sitter friend, Lillian."

In 1974, Earl Hays, Sue Bennett College president for about thirty years, established a folk festival to celebrate the folk arts, crafts, and entertainment found in the mountains of eastern Kentucky. At one of the first festivals, Hays was photographed with Sue Bennett music professor Jeanne Wintringham. The photograph was made by Don Chesnut, as were the next seven in this series.

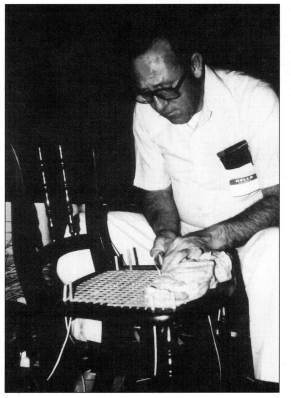

Carl Campbell was an enforcement officer for the Kentucky Department of Transportation, but his avocation was recaning chairs, a venerable mountain craft. Here he is shown at one of the first Sue Bennett Folk Festivals. The festivals continued for twenty years.

John Carpenter may be London's modern "renaissance man." He is an athlete, engineer, photographer, author, equestrian, and friendly fellow. Here he is shown at one of the SBC Folk Festivals with his display of photographs at the festival's photograph competition.

Face painters at the folk festival usually attracted children. But when this photograph was snapped, festival committee members Sis Griffin (left) and Ann Smith may have been celebrating their second childhoods. The folk festival attracted thousands of Laurel County students during its five-day run each April.

Pete House was a retired commercial pilot and a veteran of World War II, having been a Japanese prisoner of war on Battaan. In retirement, he took up jewelry making. Here he is shown at one of the Sue Bennett College Folk Festivals.

Bard Conyer and a friend watched Jim Sams carve a duck decoy at one of the annual festivals. Sams has sold the hand-carved decoys locally as well as nationally. Talk-show host Johnny Carson has purchased his decoys.

The Old Timey Hymn Sing opened the Sue Bennett Folk Festival on Wednesday night each year. Here Charles Gabbard, a former county clerk in Laurel County, is shown as he conducted a shaped-note singing school at the hymn sing one year at the festival.

Quilting bees are traditions in the mountains, and each folk festival had a quilting demonstration. This photograph shows from left to right: Sarah Sparks, Edna Green, and Edith Ponder. The woman standing is unidentified. The ladies usually made a few stitches in the quilt they were working on, but much of their time at the festival was spent talking about quilting, or anything else, with passers by.

This aerial view of Sue Bennett College's campus was made sometime in the early 1970s. College Street is in the foreground, and West Fifth runs along the right side.

The collections of Irene Isaacs and Steve Dalton each yielded this photograph of the Laurel County Fairgrounds sometime in the 1920s. The fairgrounds moved from the Camp Ground area to the land on top of Town Hill on Whitley Street, to the Broughton property on North Main Street, then to the property on US 25 south of London where the London Rotary Forms plant is now.

This photograph from the collection of Coralie Young shows a bus operated by the London & Corbin (bus) Line, the predecessor to the Black Bus Line, which eventually became the Black Brothers Bus Line. This photograph was made probably before 1927, when O.H. Black established his company and bought the permits of the earlier company. Neither the driver nor the passengers were identified.

This photograph was labeled simply, "At the old fairground in London, KY." The persons lined up on the platform were not identified, but appear to be perhaps a Girl Scout or Campfire Girls troop. The style of clothing seems to indicate that the photograph was made sometime in the 1920s.

This photograph may be of a trotting race at the fairgrounds at the Camp Ground location. It is not identified, but matches in some ways other photographs made at the fair.

The Laurel County Homecoming programs were traditionally begun with the playing of "The Star-Spangled Banner" each year, with either the London National Guard unit or Civil Air Patrol cadet squadron furnishing the color guard. This photograph from about 1969 shows the CAP color guard. The only member who can be identified is Ronnie Webb (far right).

That same year at the Laurel County Homecoming, London radio newsman Jim Parman was broadcasting live from the event on the station's mobile unit, KK-5085. Here he interviews Caren Maxwell. Parman was an announcer at WFTG each morning for about a decade. According to Parman's watch, the photograph was made at 5:35 pm.

Fires plagued London's downtown area for much of its early history. These photographs appear to be of the Jackson Building fire in October 1908. The building, on the corner of North Main and West Fourth Streets, still stands, having been repaired after the fire. It currently houses the law offices of Elmer and Willis Cunnagin and Melvin Vaughn's London Insurance Agency. It is apparently the oldest building in downtown London, having been first constructed by W.S. Jackson in about 1874 and then destroyed by fire in about 1885. It was rebuilt from bricks taken from the first building as well as from the recently-razed first Laurel County Courthouse. In the lower photograph, a safe and heating stove are in the middle of West Fourth Street. (From the collection of Irene Isaacs.)

This photograph may be of furniture and other property taken from the Jackson Building fire in 1908. It appears to be of Main Street looking north from about the southeast corner of Main and Fourth Streets.

A year later the Stillwell Hotel burned on West Fifth Street. This photograph "by Benge" shows not the hotel, but the material taken from the building to save it from the fire. The street in front of Sparks' Feed Store is Broad. It shows (left) a tailoring shop that may have been owned by a Mr. Fautz. Behind it is the spire and rear end of the St. Andrew's Catholic Church.

The front porch of the Stillwell Hotel can be seen barely through the smoke. The spire of the Methodist church, which was also destroyed in the fire, can be seen (at left) as well as the edge of the front of the Catholic church (right) with its picket fence. Note the marble-topped dresser in the bottom of the photograph.

Here we can see much of the hotel's furniture, the edge of the Lee McHargue home (left), and a better view of the Catholic church and the tailor shop, which bears the legend, "Fine Tailoring," in the window. The Stillwell Hotel was made up of the homes of A.L. Moore and John H. Jackson, which were connected by additions. (The two photographs on this page and the Jackson Building photographs are from the collection of Irene Isaacs.)

Though a well-trained and equipped volunteer fire department was established, fires continued to plague downtown. The courthouse built in 1885 was destroyed in 1958, and other businesses fell victim to the flames. **(Above)** This picture was made the morning after an explosion destroyed much of the block of East Fourth Street between Main and Hill Streets in January 1978. (From the collection of Linda Wayne Reep.) **(Below)** An early 1970s fire destroyed the Burger Queen restaurant in Carnaby Square. The business was rebuilt and eventually the business name changed to Druther's.

As the fire department increased its training regimen and improved its equipment, the number of fires in downtown began to decrease. This photograph shows the fire department's first use of its aerial ladder truck, fighting a fire in the Pica Building, which housed Poynter's Western Tool and Automotive's S&T Hardware Store. The structure was rebuilt and now houses Carousel Florist, a law office, a travel agency, and an accounting firm.

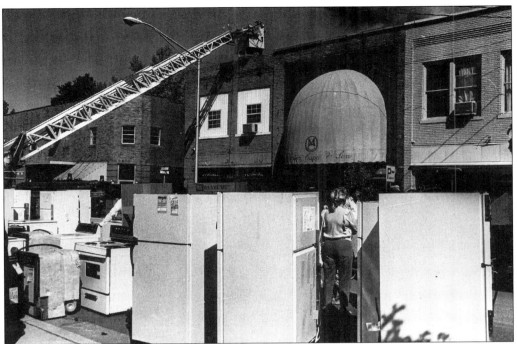

About a year later, at homecoming time, a fire damaged the building owned by Martin Cupp Furniture, which had frontages on both Hill Street and Main Street. The fire also damaged the office of Dr. Sam Tryee, some apartments, and Barton's Jewel Box, seen beneath the bucket on the aerial ladder.

After a fire on Election Day, November 4, 1973, volunteer fire fighter Pete O'Dell stopped in the Laurel County Courthouse to vote.

Showing off their new firetruck in October 1974 are the members of the London Fire Department. From left to right, firemen are as follows: (seated in the cab) Bob West; (standing) Wilson Rawlings, Kermit Parker, Lawrence McClain, Rick Dupree, Herman McKnight, Bo Rains, Ernie Clark, Gilmore Phelps, Albert Davis, Pete O'Dell, Charles Tharp, Bobby Massie, and unidentified; (standing on the truck) Terry Baker, J.C. Doane, Cecil Anderson, and Jim Knuckles. Other members not in the photograph were Otha Marcum, Everett Chadwell, Junior McKnight, Hershell Blanton, Jerry Cottongim, Joe Brown, Bobby Clark, Archie Eversole, Bob Gambrel, and Wayne Reep. The London Fire Department was organized in 1922.

In 1962 a fire department was organized to serve the county. This photograph was made in the early 1970s and shows, from left to right, R.C. Walker, Lawrence McClain, Gerald Robinson, Huey Watkins, J.R. Jones, Melvin McKnight Jr., Wayne Watkins, Doug Feltner, Ray Delph, and Jim Howard.

Members of the Keavy Fire Department posed about twenty years ago in front of the firehouse. From left to right are Carl Anders, Roy Arnold, Eddie Day, Ellis Hill, Luther Karr, Ronnie Bales, Sheldon Bunch, Thomas Williams, Morris Black, Jimmy Jones, Randall Cassidy, Donnie Lincks, and Foyster Cassidy. Others not shown were Vernon Karr, Everett Karr, Paul Kilbourne, and Curtis Young. The department was organized in 1971.

The East Bernstadt Fire Department was organized in 1965. Shown in front of the department's headquarters building in 1975 are, from left to right, Randall Adams, Cecil Isaacs, Elmer, Roger, Ed and Lincoln Schott, Bradley Moore, Charles Riley, Wayne Watkins, Mike Waldroff, Bob Hurley, J.R. Jones, Howard Reed, Huey Watkins, Billy Rice, Lonnie Baker, Alton Hansel, Raymond Roark, Lawrence McClain, and Ed Hensley. Not shown were George Harrison, W.E. McQueen, Donnie Schott, James Wickers, C.B. Hurley, and Jack Anders.

The London Firemen's Band was organized in 1932 and seldom passed up a chance to perform. This photograph shows the band at an unidentified event, probably soon after it was organized.

These two photographs, probably made on the same day in 1935, show the Firemen's Band in marching formation. The upper photograph shows the band on Main Street perhaps in the block north of Seventh Street. One store (left) has a sign plugging electrical supplies in its left window and the legend, "D.L. Woodward Groceries," in its right window. The lower photograph shows the band marching west on West Fifth Street in front of the home of D.C. Edwards, now the location of St. William's Catholic Church. Members of the band were: Rufus Bruner (drum major), Elmer Williams, Bill Ormsby, Earnest Muster, Tommy Watkins, Bill Conley, Walter Dyche, James Bowles, Jimmy Williams, Jack Rogers, Martin Dyche, E.A. Childress, Paul Stewart, Hobart Bryant, Frank Edwards, Mary Elizabeth Eversole, Milroy Bruner, Reuel Buchanan, Ralph Hammack, Dillard Collier, Russell Dyche, and Philip Hodge. Others in the band were John L. Bruner, George Hamm, and William L. Bruner. (Both from the collection of R.J. Bruner.)

London has been the headquarters site for the Kentucky State Police and the Kentucky Highway Patrol from the inception of the state police service. In 1958 Trooper Harold Watson posed with his new cruiser and displayed the emergency equipment carried by the Kentucky State Police, which was organized in the late 1940s to replace the highway patrol. In the lower photograph on the same day, the troopers at Post 11 posed for a group photograph. From the left are, as identified on the back of the photograph: (kneeling) Watson, Bobby Walker, James A. "Hook" Hendrickson, Coburn Richardson, James R. Herrell, Ray Brittain (or Jim Powell), unknown, and Edgar Estes; (standing) unknown, John Adams, two unknowns, Willis Martin, Raymond Hail, Harold West, Jackie Murphy, Ellis Ross, and two unknowns.

Chester Scoville was one of Laurel's most beloved citizens. By the time he retired, he had spent many years as a real estate broker. This photograph shows him as a captain in the Kentucky Highway Patrol. He had also worked for the State of Kentucky and delivered license plates to each of the 120 counties in the 1930s. Scoville served one term as Laurel County sheriff and several as Laurel County jailer. In his election campaign he used the slogan: "The Same Man Every Day"; and he advocated "putting the jelly on the bottom shelf so everyone can have a chance to get it." Even in his later years he was never without a smile and a joke. (From the collection of Janis Scoville.)

Since Prohibition was repealed, Kentucky chose local option, and Laurel County voted itself "dry" in the 1930s, making illegal liquor the bane of local law enforcement officers. In the upper photograph made in the 1960s, (from left to right) Sheriff Ray Bledsoe, Alcoholic Beverage Control Agent Jack Miller, Calvin Cummins, and KSP Detective James "Les" Yaden display a load of booze picked up in a raid. In the lower photograph, twenty years later, (from left to right) troopers Jimmy and Johnny Phelps and Tony Cambron inventory the liquor taken in a raid.

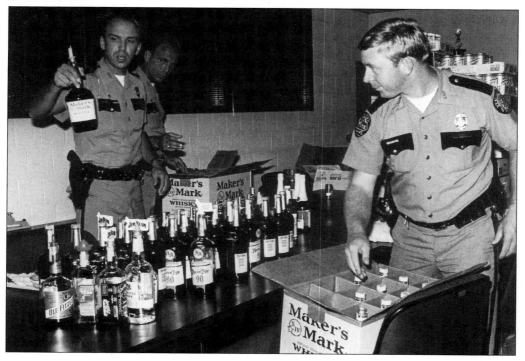

Sheriff Chester Scoville (left) and his deputy, Vic Smith, took some time out for a photograph at what appears to be a carnival sometime around 1960.

In 1978 Leslie County Judge Exec. C. Alan Muncy chose to name a new recreation center in Hyden for Richard M. Nixon, the thirty-seventh president. Nixon had resigned the presidency in shame as a result of the Watergate scandal in August 1974. The trip to Hyden at Muncy's invitation was the first public appearance by Nixon since his resignation. This photograph showing Nixon and Jailer Big John Bowling greeting each other was made in 1978 as Nixon returned from his trip to Hyden and was about to depart by aircraft from London's airport, Magee Field.

Jennings Chesnut enjoyed flying. The upper photograph shows him in about 1960 with his aircraft that was based at London's airport. He enjoyed flying so much that in later years he took up building his own aircraft as a hobby. The lower photograph shows him at work in his shop, apparently stretching fabric on the fuselage. The assistant in the rear of the shop was not identified, but could have been Fred Christian.

Three
Places in Laurel

Laurel County has lots of places to explore—historic places, recreational places, and just plain home places. The photograph above shows the home place of Charles and Nora Cook on South Main Street at Thanksgiving time in 1951. Note the stone retaining walls. The walls were removed in the spring of 1997 to make way for the widening of the street to three lanes. Charles Cook and his brother, Finley, were partners in the Cook Bros. Motor Company, founded about 1930, originally as a Pontiac dealer. (From the collection of Coralie Young.)

This is the inside of the London Post Office c. 1914. At the urging of Congressman Vincent Boreing and his successor, D.C. Edwards, the government began building a federal courthouse in London in 1908. It was dedicated in 1911. The post office was moved from the Catching Building to the new federal building and was located there until 1961, when a new post office building was built. This photograph shows, from left to right, an unidentified clerk, Bill Chesnut, and Eugene Hackney (the new postmaster). (From the collection of Irene Isaacs.)

(Above) Postmaster Eugene Hackney (right) is shown in his office with the unidentified clerk from the previous image. (Below) Postmaster Hackney (right) also posed with Bill Chesnut. Chesnut later bought an interest in Laurel Grocery Company. Hackney served as postmaster from 1914 until 1920. (From the collection of Irene Isaacs.)

Wayne and Margaret Feltner Reep and daughter, Linda Wayne, posed for this photograph in 1951. The Reeps were in the furniture business for many years at Feltner Furniture on East Fourth Street, a company founded by Mrs. Reep's father, W.R. Feltner. (From the collection of Linda Wayne Reep.)

In about April 1952, four-year-old Linda Reep (right) posed with three-year-old Dickie Doane at the Doane home on West Seventh Street. The Weaver home can be seen in the background. (From the collection of Linda Wayne Reep.)

Mattie Eversole Feltner and her husband, W.R. Feltner, were photographed in their home office in London. The Feltners were in the insurance business and had established a furniture business on East Fourth Street. (From the collection of Linda Wayne Reep.)

On graduation day in 1953, Margaret Reep, having just graduated from Sue Bennett College, posed with daughter, Linda, who had just graduated from the London Woman's Club Kindergarten. (From the collection of Linda Wayne Reep.)

Since 1826, with perhaps the exception of a few days between the destruction of the first courthouse and construction of the second courthouse in about 1885, some sort of county headquarters building has stood in the middle of town. These photographs, made in 1960, show downtown with an empty lot where the courthouse was supposed to stand. The second courthouse had burned and been razed and the third (current) courthouse was not under construction yet. The upper photograph looks east and the lower photograph looks west.

Sometime between 1908 and about 1920, these men were photographed in the late afternoon in front of the Catching Building. Note that the sidewalk is of concrete but the streets are still virtually unpaved. Behind the man on the left, a concrete crosswalk can be seen on East Fifth Street as can a crosswalk to the left of that on Main Street. The Christian Church is in the extreme left of the photograph, as is the Wren Block.

A bit earlier in the afternoon, perhaps on the same day, these two ladies were escorted across the unpaved East Fourth Street near the southern end of the Catching Block. The sign on the post (left) indicates that there is a drugstore in the building. The photograph was probably made sometime after 1910 since the northern end of the Catching Building (which housed the Catching Hotel) is only two stories, instead of its original three. After the building burned in about 1908, it was immediately rebuilt, with the hotel portion being rebuilt with two instead of three stories.

When parking was allowed on both sides of Main Street, P.L. Young made this photograph for a postcard. The image, made in about 1950, shows, from the right, the National Bank and the Catching Building. Daniel's Department Store is shown on this end of the Catching Block. (From the collection of Sweetie Smith.)

Young also shot this c. 1950 photograph of the Laurel Hotel Building, which then housed not only the hotel, but also, at the far right, the Greyhound bus station and a cafe. On the far left, a portion of the Watkins Auto Parts building and another cafe are visible. (From the collection of Sweetie Smith.)

The empty courthouse square shown in the previous aerial photographs can be seen better in this photograph made from the roof of the Lee McHargue home on Broad Street. It shows the Catching Building, which housed the following, from left to right: Begley Drug, the Hotel London, the Laurel Dress Shop, Brock's Variety Store, Emmett Shearer Insurance, the Second National Bank, and Daniel's Department Store. The First National Bank is shown on the right.

Downtown had changed just a bit when this aerial was shot, looking west about fifteen years after the previous image was taken. The new courthouse had been completed. The public library had been remodeled and expanded. A new jail had been built, and some storefronts had changed.

London's entrances were photographed from the air about twenty-five years ago. The upper photograph is looking south on I-75 at the KY 192 intersection. The Ramada Inn can be seen at the left and across the road from it is the London Inn Shell station. Behind there is the Daniel Boone General Store. The Boggs Subdivision is visible in the upper right of the photograph.

This image shows KY 25 south of town looking north. The picture was made in about 1960, and the only commercial building visible is the roof of the Dixie Tobacco Warehouse at the very top of the photograph.

The faculty and student teachers at London Junior High were photographed in about 1963. From left to right are: (front row) Marjorie Rawlings, Eva Young, Grace Kidd, and student teacher Barbara Binder; (back row) Zack T. Banks, Jack Hendrix, Carman Weaver, and student teacher Roland Mullins. (From the collection of Linda Wayne Reep.)

London Elementary School teachers Bennie Hammons (left) and Elizabeth Young were photographed in about 1963 by Linda Wayne Reep. (From the collection of Linda Wayne Reep.)

The occasion of installing a lighted sign around 1960 at the offices of the *Sentinel-Echo* prompted the making of these photographs, but the interesting historical part of the photographs is not what was shot intentionally, but that which was photographed coincidentally. A portion of the restaurant operated for many years by Bert Edwards is shown in the upper right. The second story was an apartment house.

This image shows a young Roland Moore (lower right), who even then operated a sign company. J.B. Phelps is shown climbing the ladder, and across Broad Street can be seen one of London's taxis at what was the taxi stand up until the late 1960s. The cab indicates on the door that it is operated by the Broad Street Cab Co. Beyond that is the Phillips saddle shop.

Destroyed by fire in the early 1980s, the Assembly of God Church on West Fifth Street was built in 1944. This photograph was made in the 1970s. The church was organized in 1937 by the Rev. M.A. Jollay and was called Jollay's Church to distinguish it from London's older Pentecostal church, which was called Begley's Church. Its dwindling congregation merged in the 1980s with London's Full Gospel Tabernacle, and the building was sold to another congregation before the fire.

London's Methodist church was photographed for a postcard by P.L. Young in the 1950s before a bell had been hung in the bell tower. Other than landscaping and some other cosmetic changes, the original church building remains virtually unchanged. The Methodists in London had quite a task just getting a church building that would last. This building was built in 1910 after the earlier frame building had burned in 1909, when the Stillwell Hotel burned. Earlier Methodist church buildings had fallen victim to fires and windstorms.

The funeral business in London has seen funeral homes come and go, but the most enduring names in the business are Rawlings and House. The two merged in the late 1970s. Prior to that, they had separate locations. The photograph above shows the Rawlings Funeral Home in about 1960. (The home is currently occupied by Mr. and Mrs. John Carpenter.)

The House Funeral Home is shown as it appeared c. 1960. The men on the front porch couldn't be identified. The building shown was replaced in the 1980s with a modern facility that houses House-Rawlings Funeral Home.

Kern's Bakery was one of the first major industries to locate in London after World War II. It was opened in December 1948. Kern's distributes bread and baked goods from London all across eastern and central Kentucky. The sign seen on this photograph made c. 1960 shows a loaf of bread with slices falling from it. At night the neon tubes outlining the sign made it appear that the slices were actually in motion.

The Vortex Cafe is shown in about 1959. The cafe had been London's first gasoline station. A barbershop was located in the left side of the building. The building was razed in 1997. The structure was just north of the intersection of Moren Road and North Main Street. (From the collection of Coralie Young.)

The Reda Theatre was built by Ernie Reda in about 1947 who had by 1954 also opened a drive-in theatre with the same name. In the middle part of the next decade, the theater fell victim to the new medium called television and attendance dropped. It remained open, though, into the early 1970s. This photograph was made by Don Chesnut just months before the building was leveled by the wrecking ball less than fifty years after it was built.

For twenty years this small frame building housed Gene Thomas's State Farm Insurance agency. It was replaced in the 1980s by a modern brick building.

The Burger Boy Restaurant, started in the early 1960s, and the Krystal Kitchen, which was in business from the 1930s until the early 1970s, were the only restaurants open all night. In the 1960s the Burger Boy moved into the building that was built in the late 1950s to house the Lakeside Drive-in. This photograph shows the Lakeside Drive-in in about 1959.

This is how the Burger Boy looked in the early 1970s.

The Ideal Restaurant was operated for many years by Laddle Cottongim. The restaurant shown in this photograph was built after a fire destroyed the original. This photograph was made in 1959 and, with the exception of a mansard roof added recently, the restaurant appears today nearly as it was when built. Earl and Rosa Smith currently operate the eatery.

Roy Schott has been operating a service station on this corner for more than thirty-five years. He stopped selling gasoline in 1997 and maintains an auto repair business there. This photograph was made in about 1959.

The 1980s saw the demise of several traditions in London and Laurel County. The old-fashioned barber has just about been replaced by the hair stylist. Just before it closed, photographer Don Chesnut made these photographs of the J.L. Delph Barber Shop on East Fourth Street.

Another tradition that has passed (at least the business owners in the area hope it is passed!) is flooding in east London. This photograph, looking east, shows high water at the corner of East Fourth and Ellen Streets. The East London Restaurant is seen on the left and a flower shop is visible on the right.

Still another tradition gone is the decoration of the Laurel County Jail at Christmastime. Jailer Big John Bowling decorated the jail each year with thousands of Christmas lights during his tenure as the jailer.

East Bernstadt was once larger than London, the old-timers will tell you. Perhaps it should be said that London was once smaller than East Bernstadt. Whichever is the case, East Bernstadt was at one time the railhead and a major coal mining community. As coal began to dwindle and the railroad pushed farther south in the 1880s, East Bernstadt began to lose population. This photograph shows the Auction Barn in the early 1970s.

This image, shot at about the same time as the one above, shows the commercial section of East Bernstadt. From the right are the post office, the Auction Barn, the old Elk Hotel, and the Casteel Hardware building.

The East Bernstadt Banking Company was the forerunner of the modern business called Cumberland Valley National Bank. This photograph shows the original building on School Street in East Bernstadt.

The Casteel Hardware, shown *c.* 1970, supplied East Bernstadt's needs for LP gas as well as tools, fertilizer, seeds, nuts and bolts, and whatever the farmer, homeowner, or businessperson might need.

This photograph, also made in 1970, provides a closer look at the Elk Hotel, located on the area's main street that is paralleled by the CSX railroad tracks.

The East Bernstadt School was photographed for its 1955 school annual. It was the last year the school had a high school. The 1955 graduates were Billy Parker, Betty June Moore, Eddie Joe Brown, Audrey Cromer, Vernon Sizemore, Louise Byrd, Jack Cloyd, Roy Lee Collins, Nannie Rose Hacker, Bernith Reed, and Lorene Ryser. The high school faculty was J.W. Cook, Elsie Bowling, Richard Morgan, and Mattie Roberts. The school is the only independent school still operating in Laurel County since London School merged with the county system in 1970. (From the archives of the East Bernstadt School.)

After East Bernstadt suspended its high school, Bush, Lily, Hazel Green, and London were the only high schools in the county. They merged in 1970. This photograph shows the Bush School just after that merger.

Hazel Green High School near Hazel Patch, where Wood's Blockhouse was established to serve the settlers who were passing through Laurel County, furnished the county with championship basketball teams since its beginning. The school was established in 1921 along with Keavy as the first public high schools in the county. Hazel Green won the state championship in 1940 and played in eight state tournaments between 1933 and 1970, the year the school merged with the rest of the county system. There is currently an elementary school on the site.

The Pittsburg School was established to serve the children of the Pittsburg community, a thriving town just north of London around the turn of the century. It was, for a while, the railhead and served as a highly-productive coal mining center in eastern Kentucky. The school was converted to a Headstart facility in the early 1980s.

Felts High School merged with Lily High and left its facility as an elementary school. In the early 1990s, Lily and Felts Elementary Schools merged to form Hunter Hills Elementary School. The building has recently been converted to apartments. Felts was in the extreme southern part of the county, and Lily was just north of it.

A bit farther north, Sublimity School, an elementary school, was established. It was the result of the consolidation of Falls, Owsley, New Sharon, and Old Union Schools in 1959.

The Rough Creek School on KY 80 east of London was one of the last two-room schools operated in the county. Its students eventually joined the pupils at Bush School, farther east. This site is currently used as a maintenance center for the school system.

The Johnson School on McWhorter Road was established in 1959 as the result of the consolidation of Johnson, Macedonia, Old Salem, Pleasant View, Twin Branch, McWhorter, Long Branch, Terrills Creek, Creech, White's Chapel, Langnau, New Salem, and Old Way.

The Keavy High School was short-lived because it didn't meet the standards of the state's department of education. The Keavy Elementary School was established in 1950 as the consolidation of Locust Grove, Keavy, Holly Grove, Oak Ridge, and Storms. That consolidation and the installation by the state highway department of signs pointing the way to the Keavy community fueled speculation in the early 1950s that the Atomic Energy Commission was eyeing Keavy as the possible site for an "atomic plant." The rumors were reportedly unfounded.

The Camp Ground School in southern Laurel County alongside KY 229, reportedly the route of the Wilderness Road, was a consolidation of Camp Ground, Laurel River, Mount Olivet, Robinson, Merrimac, Union, and Cane Creek Schools. The Camp Ground area was one of the earliest settled parts of the county, and legendary Methodist circuit rider Bishop Francis Asbury held revival meetings there.

The Colony Elementary School is at Bernstadt, a settlement peopled by the Swiss in the 1880s. The modern school is the result of the 1950 merger of Lower Colony, East Colony, Upper Colony, Liberty, Flat Rock, and Sunny Rock.

This photograph shows the Upper Colony School. The teacher was Mrs. Schalch. The image is from the collection of Eddie Binder, who is seated second from the right on the bench.

The "Swiss Colony," established as and still called Bernstadt, has brought many fine families into Laurel County, families with that Swiss pride and thrift that made the land bloom. Family names such as Muster, Fiechter, Schott, Binder, Meyer, Krahenbuhl, Konizer, Ryser, Keller, Abbuhl, Huber, Ulrich, and Zimmerman are scattered all over the county as the result of their ancestors who took a chance on Laurel County, boarded a ship, and moved here. Mr. and Mrs. Arnold Schuepbach (picture here) came to Laurel County with their parents from Bern. They are the ancestors of the Binder family. Their daughter, Bertha, married John V. Binder. (From the collection of Eddie Binder.)

Ed Binder, son of John and Bertha Binder, is shown with his dog in front of the Schuepbach home at Bernstadt. He was the father of retired auto dealer Eddie Binder. (From the collection of Eddie Binder.)

John U. Binder posed with his wife, Bertha (right), and his daughter Dorrinda (center). John and Bertha Binder were also the parents of Francis, Loucille Binder Cornett, John, Ed, Lewis, and Delbert. (From the collection of Eddie Binder.)

The Delbert Binder family posed about the time of World War II in the studio of Herman Mullins. Delbert and Ethel "Mom" Binder are pictured here with their children, Alvin, Kenneth, Virginia, Keith, and Maurice. (From the collection of Virginia Binder Bowling.)

The congregation of the Swiss Colony Baptist Church posed in front of the original stone church building in the 1950s. That building was soon replaced with a modern brick structure near the site of the Swiss Reform Church.

The Binder family, as were most of the Swiss who settled in the "Colony," were excellent husbandmen of the soil and natural resources. This is the mule team used by the Binder Lumber Company *c*. 1950 to transport logs from the woods to the sawmill.

The workers of the Binder Lumber Company were photographed in 1946. From left to right are: (front row) Junior Sullivan, Robert Jones, Edd Binder, Bleve Jones, John Brummitt, Walter Oakley, and Fred Shaffer; (back row) D.O. Binder, Jimmie Wells, Cape Jones, ? Casteel, Lewis Binder, Walter Johnson, Bill Jones, John Keller, and Arthur Wagers. (Both photographs from the collection of Virginia Bowling.)

This photograph shows a 1944 view of one of the Binder Lumber Company's sawmills.

The Binder brothers were not only in the lumber business, but also the automobile business. This 1950s photograph shows, from left to right, the brothers who owned the local Buick dealership: Ed, Lewis, Delbert, and Francis.

London's St. Andrew's Catholic Church and School became St. William's once a combination new school and church building was built in 1954. It was renamed for Archbishop William O'Brien, of the Church Extension Society. The sixth grade at St. William's School posed on the front porch of the church in April 1955. Listed alphabetically, they are Lois Ann Blunschi, Frank DeMarcus, Lawton Hounchell, Gene Gill, Virginia Sue Powell, Donald Reda, Paul Richenburg, and Sandra Sparks. (From the collection of Geedle Jody Peters.)

The Sue Bennett Training School provided high quality education for London's children into the 1950s. This photograph of a second grade class was made in the 1949/50 school year and shows (seated) James Wilson Brooks, Jakie Wittenback, Johnny Jones, and Robert Early. The first three standing girls were not identified; the next three are Nancy Whittenback, Geedle Jody, and Alice Ann Tucker. The last girl was not identified. (From the collection of Geedle Jody Peters.)

The names of the sisters in this photograph were not remembered, but students at the vacation Bible school at the St. Andrew's Church in the early 1950s were: (front row) Mary Louise O'Neal, Judy Weaver, Steve Morris, Mary Ann Shuler, and Ricky Curry; (second row) Geraldine O'Neal, Mike Reda, and Eddie Freeman; (third row) not identified except for Geedle Jody, the last on the row; (fourth row) Bill Shuler, Jerry Weaver, Don Reda, and Johnny Jones; (fifth row) Peggy Jones, unknown, Pat Higgs, unknown, and Jakie Hackney. (From the collection of Geedle Jody Peters.)

John and Lou Miller were photographed in the 1960s at their home on the Marydell Road. He was a farmer, and she, a homemaker. They reared seven children: John R. Miller, Beatrice Miller Smith, Lettie Miller Smith, Pauline Miller Dyke, Hazel Miller Barnard, Evelene Miller Greene, and Daisy Pearl Miller Greene.

W.T. "Shorty" and America Greene were photographed in the early 1950s at their home on Dyche Street. They came from Winchester to London in 1942, when Mr. Greene was employed by Mark Watkins at his wholesale auto parts company. He worked as an on-the-road auto parts salesman for both Watkins and himself until his retirement in the early 1960s. Mrs. Greene was active in the children's department at London's First Baptist Church and Corinth Baptist Church. They reared four sons, William Thomas Jr., Henry, Carl G., and Perry Greene; and two daughters, Joan Greene Brown and Mary Frances Greene House.